HERODIAS

HERODIAS

✝

MICHAEL RANK

CHORALE EDITIONS

ISBN 0-9708586-7-1

With the priest's tongs --

ISAIAH

✢   ✢   ✢

Occult horse.

The cutlery. Tarn's pilgrimed;
We ingest the watered room.
tongue grid. The Ram now subject to Lot's clay
will gesture/ Sun elapse, venous.
I am cause ------------- vault decay.

carriage song

+   +   +

Lexicon: sounding lords
Ligament: this bandage it robs. clerestory.
Priest: A motion ✳
Resin: column, Tarn's lodge

+   +   +

Circus, shallots, ochre:
        Burial impede.
    It must breathe in fraction.
------ (confederates)   Sentinels Ag
   And wasp. The axle drags as charm.

+   +   +

Minotaur
entreates procession and sway.
the wax head will tour in sign:
[Absolve
[Dissolve
[Dismay / Assassinate.

Customs, antlered pass.
Vomits the underbay. And incants
eye (asp)
Tar / witness.

✛　　✛　　✛

Come silence,
The menagerie is god
Sparkle fish (and whore)
I am arabic orchard
Above. betrothed.

+   +   +

Diadem tasks among the shavings, vacant
with mare and kite.
: Meter converts arm, (to badge)
exception follows gate
wreathing.

+ + +

We have begun to separate. Mermaid.
I will steal your hands
change to Name
lost consulting the marks.

This is Torso ✳ To signify

+   +   +

             Sacrament collars the sun
Systems.
       Of wedding preserved
through alkaline tanks. Documents
tonic and sign; the watch,
           dark. Owls.

+   +   +

Trumpets   Withering cage.
Absinthe to synapse hound: Emaciated
restoring song. You will come binding Apostle's work.

Loud's greatest fragment.

+   +   +

Comes rope
    pulls to rib cage: hull, oak, and dung.
    sediment flower
    Mansions   (nitrate)spoon.

+   +   +

Sun bless to Father's arm.
     The mansion is oaring, and colour
        with sage, cyclical station {lament, Kaspar
  / Ox aim

pregnance, crowning Loud's caul.

    ✛   ✛   ✛

Aegis, scholars curtain.
The savage, hearing glass. Through
conscious placement of stone;
corrosive sent
and cord.
The Magi's cancer dream
Theseus axis.

+   +   +

I am gleaning from the Apothecary's waist.

+   +   +

The led of control is a throwing. Adhere,
contagious flood. Arms set back
in counting wonder.
stencil of seethe,
alliance culture.
The toppling of whore is assist.
I will display veins.

+   +   +

Acid tasks, acquires: of storm.
a pleading wills permanence in dye.
I am starving the kill.
Negative leagues
Medicant kind
To tragic. To tragedy.
Binds Dyer's climb in degrees of salve.

Codex salve as point of God.

+   +   +

Speeds head

I love you
horse
as Astarte.

I am sent for the chapel, "seven incisions of breath." A charted sleeve
bereaves me and is suspect: The anatomy of Christians water
                    The dogshead Simon displays.
Husk. Iluminate asps odious measure. Spits rattle offers tarn/ Breeds
ladderings of Fly. I taste lost dosage To retrieve And aspect rind.
All the mentions are unclear, staggered in iron and bloods. I am grace born.
Wrapped in oaring.
                    Binary lords.   The Oxen Blind ●
                                        Sacrifists. Sacrificial.
The envoy lays broken in rope, framed by the wool and flies of ether.
A parchment and a wave are diagramed to his side. We will find you this
way, in a clearing; a Lion of stain to gather those bled and displace the chapel
floor.
            {And the sky will not be named, as damage is above.

It was well into morning when they sunk his eyes. The bottom lids filled
with golden paste. Some water. He had been kept from the table until the last
sweeping frost. How ritual forgives its seams.   \The containment was drawn
from inks of the flood. Intersecting in ankles and hands. In charcoal
relief the image strays. Unfixed to our crimes; we have seen a solace.
The subsequent wars remain to wooden icons
    With haloes line my neck.
To gilded page, recites of disease. The slaughter promises a pale newborn horse.
Harvest, I am loathsome prayer: ------{sage, crucifix.

A motion of heavens deform, wades Antlered and Named.
            Lot's witness lies carving.

With onyx and forceps; aluminum patterned charge. Each habit an
emerald blue. The chording of scripture.   The garden we would find
ourselves in sat removed. Locked in hands, in these circles around him,
the nettles fell from our mouth.   A graft. A bridal ring.
                    We reigned from the laps of statue; overlooked
back fielded wire. The jewelry we had bound hung in clusters, reeds.
Spotting our hair and remains.
                    Delivers ---------------- Spire(s)
            And your oracle bled the grounds, admitting a haloed snow.
            The lamias sinking eye; tones of russet and bone.
Bandage, less honored in frieze as we are led to sea]
                    The side of christ's horn./ A magnificence of trees.
As I were to arms bent; hands clustered off side my heart. With fingers
lodged in design ,ward old intents.
And bounding, I place toward of misgiving; and all such difficult space.

The straw parting to our side, clearing you crosses of beach. Bands to you
the tow of yellowed groves, brine. This wreck carve and moored below
the thrones of Sebastions mission; steered west come such that we near in day/
        Reptile and faulted.
And the commons and forgiven fall to the ore, while birth holds settled
with resolve. Drowned dear to ether and stone; in approach of throne unmarred.
                House of Christian offered to tar.
Had we fed less than this, I have forgotten the ways.   In design
of starground, the herdings outreaches the throne. As we try past the eyes
of such storm~ praying mingle to the shifts of calm, as listless to our knees.
        Vanished by speech and sail and pardon.
        The abundance sees us rooming through some sea.
                        A paramount of holly. Sedates
the powdered toll; as binds our cheek and eye. Centers off the spoil
we are the last confidence of sand: That which honours in Robe,
                        stagnant sparrowed wine.
As we strive to recall, the life lines blur. Half-remembrance; as in song.
Lifting us down the trees, we swept out the tinned grass
        and stepped into the day.
They lay bent to the roofs, wounded in the speak.
The saddens were shorn of the leopards train. Dragging in the drifts
that found her. Dismantled in anchor, we arc to the gold. Flagging oars
to dot the rust.   Higher, the stillness impairs in reverence. An attic whore;
lurches of Rome. Heirs through wound iron steps/the son dining from sign.
This we keep near.
Louds house as cage, as Dyers ark. Crossed, our backs
will last a white line.   They approach me with palms displaced. Saturns
of rouge; minerals to dry the shine. A wretch that abhors she, one straps the
pleated ground. Unfed the watered drawing to lure us,
                The cross's sleeping eye.
This landscape knows forgiveness of ruptured time. Attracts to fallen kind.
                Centurions. My stunted less breath.
Their arms came through watered cloud. From in a reddened floor of the sea.
As pearl placed their nails, touched to our misgiving.
                                Our hoods remain inherit
House of Christian   To the Batteries sick.

                +   +   +

And revere one hundred bough. Celestite(as)weariness. The charted sleeve
routing all we know. This speak of deliverance now habits the crew,
suggesting an hour of light.
       Our ankles west and bound. Resurrected, harnessed
remove. Gleaming the rights before us,
          embroidered of the limb. A circle fossil line flanks the wise.
          ------- Saline and encoded.]
Heralding, as Christians eyes labyrinth with the blind. Our steps are token skin.
Of repetition I amend.
All is of Bast, and dilate.   I anoint the drift/points of cross, and wait.
The rigging, a hierarchal emblem to offer me complete of gods will.

Dyers gothik cage: As hanging and tablet.

Coronation; a quarterdeck of fly(s).   The sovereigns lattice king.
I am marked the cloud sub crown will bring.
        Heather and babtil wreath.
Christian fed among the Pyrates,
misplaced to the altars fumes. The eyes we've filled down gold.
Their crew wept and staggered, bowed doused in higher rags. Redden.
Bested in twine, Christian falters to his knees. Shipmarks and tools.
   The Gold in alcohol.
   Herod bled the sails and writhed for the reefs;
          His arms gone purple from the sun.
If there is salt I can no longer tell.   The Waterfield stands witness.
    This as pronounced to Dyer: The serum Kaspar wept.
And whites of the water blot this oceans skin. Removed of mud and delay.
His crew pains the vaults with lion and buds; drawn of heavens determination,
set down in haggard sky. Willed, the glass beached us to home.
A gift, drone wretched waves. In the space I bled, wrought true harms bows;
a lack you damaged sound\   I admit to all the dyes. A drift that suggests to ether.
          Points latitude of the drown.
The Pyrates raptured toward the terrace. These sails blinding to the rim.
Adorned its dead, the golden hull spat across the stone. Grinding perfume
to our eyes.   Herod wrapped himself in cloud and dove from the mast
         His wings seared in glare as he fell.

       +   +   +

These stations of loss now define elliptic tribe.
                                        Hours of soil: A charting
which alphabets/sign O. Our guide breathes muzzles crown, laps at the
continents before us. The toxins in belief nurture to solid ground
                        Plantation, I have little resist.
This lexicon will drown us; spares our lips, and bows.
With song we willed hallucinate out shifts of devotion [Such accomplices
delve past sutures and line.
        Fins of the Ram
I await the frozen, knowing ash of wonders spine.
Unsure casts this drift blooded maze
    [I am gift,
    [all despise   I will rake the flowered born.
My hands are alone; parting with invent.
Herods birds rise slain through smoke   Retching violents gold.
We wait the crimes to hold us. Nears of tatters,
                                        shoal.
I forgive only your rime. The missions baked in sun.

                    Witch. Artery. A circle sustains three;
                                        and legion.
                    Carriage is to print with wine,
            chapters of whiteness.   Asp. Left subject to Arcs fin.

The shroud wept with sail. Held blood of honoured beacons.
And the betrays voice in word; lose all repair.   /There are two to hide me.
This Mass as beginning, as harm to wonders bled. In peace,
as captures myths wall.
        To astound; wed beautiful space, And reborn.
The cattle should not be near this pilgrim{stake,
                            cattle arch and guide.
The stained man chants ochre to the sun: as in pray. And leads us into war}
As armor dog/gifts to the mouth, lifts to plagues imprint. Within ravage,

    to all Sub Gold.
I retrieve in awe of such savage letting; as though we had yet to arrive,
                            of glorious wave, and decline.

            +   +   +

The beheading was to sleep for Simons days : fire had been altered.
And how Hyenas sigilled name, of chorale and paste,
are songs to contact the limb.
At cost we wandered close now. Christians marks hatched the bay.
[ward old intent]   Forgiven the coming of this lord
Forgiven the day.
And they waste about the stones. Trailing
drift comb, rots of hair. Winter subdues our claim.
The Goat as sternum,
Incantation and refusal.   I conceive in charts of Rome.
assemblage of boat and botanist
Adhesive throat.
This alchemy beads to the sulphur, a wreath
down our hands. We are given to below.
Lot's dwelling in cable
I am on stems
This accent
(This) Grail
{His Pyrates sprawl to the vats.
Railing to the trees, lords silicate weight. The letters of rebirth.
A static weather splayed in wave
Symbols the tar soaked wave.
Kinds pregnant in fall. Streaked, and skins run.
The taste surrenders no extinction.   I willed step ----------- And vanish.
We have stitched wings to our daughters back. Fastening the offerings with hooks
and jewels. We will crayon their eyes and leave them to the spires.
Our daughters/
Hunters a scarlet mine, the tapestries known of fathers war. A conflict of
eyes and the crime. The soil more precious than gold. Your pages gathered insist
with encoded motes; tortures of holy air.
This breed will define the Sheperds tomb/ A weapon of coal standing life.

Throughout the broken bodies, Mars guards
the trees impair.

+   +   +

The burials streak, and black objects crown the diggers face. With removal
I offer winged and rope; as binding to rapture lords eye .
   Our chidren have been absent for all their time.   The Hanging Bells
                                             Embedded in rows.
Simon: as collapsed to the autumns floor, bleeding from out hands
and bliss. Cradled to the glow of our rotten/ He seeks to higher sounds.
Untracked as the arch paves, I resist all spoken.
                                 To kind.   The bark fixed
with buds; your nineteen animals wander through the keep.
The funerals now hang to our hips. Markers
placed rusted through sand. His landings burnt with circles and puddled
of zinc.   Kissing those witnessed like a crown. \The beautiful snow feeding
to hand.   And silence repents all we are showing. A sanded carnal law.
Red notes dashed aground in altar; artifact to our Sisters fall.
I offer believes: And the white obscures us. Damaged, uncharting stone.
          The bodice of shipwreck.}
Under fathoms of clay the haulers drift and sieve. Spelled drums
beating out the ice. They oar faded machines locked in pearl and finds.
In regard of alien way -----------< a forgotten home.
   [The remnant stretched its hands, and wandered passed our reach.
   [Christians court filling the sky.
The visitation asks of gift. Circumferenced measure, bent in scratch, aligns
the tropics floor. I am disband: our wholesome claim.
                          Downs suffocate in design. Unmerited;
blest uncure. Left to allay the sulfur
                           Ra's wounded tooth.
It was still so dear, slows calcified. I catch at rays as unscalding/ unseen amounting
shiver. Belie the dyes. Is with coast and edifice scrying our undoing knows of love.
The removes a violet crawl, an etch you will wound miles of cast.
   I howls miss, this optic tribe   And stills carnival,
                   reluctant from the wars.

                +   +   +

The doors are Lot's immersion. Base metals and rum. In searing of the vestis
will deny a progress: Ides fortune, combs the sun.
                            Rats shelter ides the sun.   This is to swarm/to negate intent
And follows a hybrid wall as Text.
He fell to us a bruised space tare. A cosmonaut breathing in flowers. Blooming
from his wrist. We bathe in his minerals and drift; set apart from this helmeted
dust. Far from Christians antlered sway.
            The bark he carries inks in sigil;
        measurements towards a blasted dome.
As warsign bands benevolent, I am riddled with pray.
                    Of children.
                    Of repair.
I loot in fallen rows. {Λ gods kiss of smile, An eye I rear your betray.
The Rams wash is subtle to the snow.   With mythic keepers: In wire decease
                                    I ache from your sounds.
This hideous summer stakes the bandaged sun. Flocked in weights of Gold,
Simon lays recovered to the fall. Knots his hand in lint >
A vaulted cruel, pyre ceremony lasts to the halls, swims carbon bowed relief
and tops into the flood.   / To jewelry of hope becoming with solid, aligned
from castled weep.   Cast in rhythmic horse {---war steeped to mud.
I wish it upon me.   Obelisk ● Erosion.   This imprint I wear as your ring.
It was not a garden to Fathers remain, the bowl at our feet spilling locust
and twine. Emergence of Ra's issue. I have dreamt of an awkward time.
                    Their wrists crossed, lapped the trees and bound /
Displays the soldiers in broken. Herodias white, tasks the walls. Departure
must be thick. The stairs unwound in totem and scar. Such heroes blue amend
the tides. Blazed aztec. And starven.   Our refraction blind the seer.

I am told you will now rest.   A chemist keeps your gown, as witness to the stain.

                            The throat as Kaspars spur.

            +   +   +

With hooves of prophet I keep watch through your side. Respiration,
addered plumes. A crowning, as fixed tropics vow saint and stride;
                                        to dilute.
The greater halls were no longer fabric. This drift of properties sees objects
unsure.   A vine of Host escapes the throat, and idles into pray.
            Surgical, and imperial embrace.
The lime would find us amazed, and rightful in design. Lines of rust to
assassinate the sway: >A coded shark to breed my take.
Coda, the sea horn has replaced your eyes; from the green of forehead.
Commons\under torch, assigned. It was not for Simon to tender Heaven
                                        By lash.
Nearing an end, the woods had threaded the windows. Battled from the
walls. We gorged in branches; our heroes steepled in the thicket.
Simon rose, crowned with drags of rope. His descent forgave this pollution}
What they are holding is unclear. Carts
                Tarns wing.   The scavengers arm:
                    The Riding jaw.✸
She is not so young that I cannot breathe; what letter I possess.
The roots of the house shed down before him, rolling off from the drown.
Stitched among the vines, fingers and torches littered as nests. Simon wept
through the tares and gathered his rings. {The tombs fell all around him.
            We will part as tamers.   Maps of egypts Gate.
                It must inflict.   Stations.

                    ✝   ✝   ✝

I have ingest the fragment, and wait by the cellars. The priests coppering lord
suspends the head.
I am as Sebastion, kindling the ill, in preparation of heavens tribe.
The battle was incomplete; to have blind the carnage saint. A measure
of Dyers return. In blessing all manner of clay
I will side this watered throne. Untasked.
Herod whispers in tryst; carving black, out runes. His feet are caked
with wish. Leaning back through lines of storm.
The stake of his thoughts
slowed due course, and shifted in blocks of sand. A rattle coughing to the stairs
as we near. He circles the strewn in cloud and waste, humming as his fingers
tap black the room. Our approach is through rust and wheels:
Simon falters past the yard,
a world away.
House of Christian   To the Batteries sick.
With riders and science bound undertow, our bearings wed out and begin.
In this I have yellowed closure.   Possession to bleed canons tour.
Herod howls through the domes
Laboring strings and trails of his headdress/
Flapping through the red sound
of sheets and belief.
As we stooped in view   of such precious a fall.

✝   ✝   ✝

The blood was of Konrads design. Terminals as wax.
Sebastion,(in dying). With copper, stage, and block}
I place the crown of trees and willed deface your calling.
        Constance.
The bark of my thighs. Your devices
are replaced with nothing.   As below, I alchemise
                                    wife: the severing host.
This land will appease in throne, and startle all gifts to clay.
From Triangle___Red lines crossing out the door. The relics at our feet
have come through draughts of leaves, and snare wide the cold.
Lapsing to the hounds, the air stalls in coils.
                                    Herod knots his leg, stirs
behind us. Scraping blades at the wheat.   Clasping himself
across the floor. Foregone, the pigeons fall in flight.
        As grey magick rescinds.

        This last fetching Cross.

The sons casket eaves the topping walls:
All manner of leaves are skinned to guide us.
The scriptures specific,
                    As with drugged. Nine points
                    Of sky I offer the spine.
                        As such weapons haul through me,
To my knees all is swept found ruin. Littering a civility left at this
hem; conscious to a blacken of bride. A downpour,
this crush recalls to an unbearable king.
        With streamers cast me out; by all kept tatters,
            founding tide. I remain forgotten.

The retchings crossed in paint/
A crypt lorn and becoming, I am dubious to the wave.
The tigers blissed in their word:
I enact all I have said. Shadowing such
departure, the animals will labor wine.

     I immerse in East walls
        ❄
     I contact unbled.

This, a dugout.   A conceive of fatal doe.
          (A) kinder throat.
                      Waxed
from wintering and cypress; our hands convince black prints.
The rain imagines us spared and whitened.
I have leaned calm to sea, expectant: As Orion.
Of vows. {And Titans reef, my hounded Moor.
     I still in turn, once again,
     for the diagram is honest.
And I haven't the dead   To this Nine
                     To Nile.
         Trophy / Borne
        Submerge the dogs
      East, Teat.   Sectioned holly
        Digestive Mast-------
With this kill, the Bride will rise founded.
   There is damage I must speed
          Of God
      And Tireless friends.
The coughing wheel   The vowelled breast.
    Arcs witches speak of Heather

        louds hymn.

        ✝